# MODERN KLOSE-LAZARUS
## Comprehensive Course for Clarinet

THE *Modern Klose-Lazarus*, a comprehensive course for clarinet, represents a compilation of two of the world's most famous clarinet methods, completely revised, re-edited and re-styled to meet the demands of modern education. The original editions of these justly celebrated works, abounding in a wealth of valuable material that for over half a century proved itself indispensable in clarinet study, were written at a time when teaching procedures were quite different from what they are today, and as a result, any attempt to make use of them in our present scheme of education inevitably results in a multitude of problems confronting students and teacher alike. Originally intended for pupils whose interests were paramount enough to justify them spending countless hours of each day in serious practice, the original versions of these great works advance in strides far too rapid for most students. Furthermore, the material as presented in the original dress of these two methods is not graded progressively; the first pages of each book are of a difficulty far beyond most beginners, and when proceeding through the two methods it is found that while the musical content is easy enough to digest in some places, in others it is completely out of bounds for those at that particular stage of advancement. Likewise, a lack of sufficient material for study in the low register of the instrument, as well as the absence of any logical presentation of studies or exercises to assist elementary players in mastering the intricacies of getting "over the break," i.e., going from the Low (Chalumeau) to the Middle (Clarion) Register of the clarinet, offer drawbacks that are sufficient to discourage the most ambitious of pupils. Then too, melodic material in the form of well-known melodies, which is so necessary in sustaining students' interest while developing the mere mechanical aspects of musical performance, does not exist among the pages of either Klose or Lazarus. These facts convinced the writer that time was opportune for a complete revision and adjustment of the two greatest of all clarinet methods, in order to bring them to a place where they could be of some real service to the students of today as well as be adaptable to either individual instruction or the class method plan of teaching.

IN the present volume the writer has directed all efforts toward modernizing and improving the original versions of Klose and Lazarus. Many new and worthwhile studies, exercises and etudes have been incorporated into the work, and in places, complete new sections have been added, given over to such problems as hitherto remained untouched. Many familiar melodies have been interspersed throughout the array of technical material, and each of the most frequently played major and minor keys is taken up in a systematic, logical fashion. Throughout the whole of the *Modern Klose-Lazarus*, constant stress is made of the absolute necessity of the regular practice of long, sustained tones, which are in themselves of prime importance to all in developing a fine tone quality, trueness of pitch, and strength of embouchure, but which, unfortunately, are so often neglected in clarinet study.

THE failure of practically all clarinet methods to offer some kind of systematic approach in the development of tones in the high register of the instrument is a weakness that has proved itself a real handicap to those desirous of attaining anything comparable to a first class technical proficiency in playing. With this thought in mind, a special section of the *Modern Klose-Lazarus*, devoted to the high register of the clarinet, introduces the art of cross-fingering in an organized, step-by-step fashion, laying much stress on the playing of long, sustained tones in the upper register of the instrument, and thus enabling students to become as skilful in manipulating this part of the clarinet as any other.

THE current work is admirably suited for class instruction in schools and its use therein will bring to the young musicians of America an opportunity to profit from the study of valuable teaching materials, devised and written by two of the greatest masters of the clarinet that the world has ever known, but which have hitherto been inaccessible to a large number of students due to their former manner of presentation.

AS a companion book to the Modern Klose-Lazarus, the writer has prepared a completely revised and modernized edition of the famous Pares exercises for clarinet, which is titled the *Modern Pares* and is published by Rubank, Inc. It is strongly urged that when students have completed the section on Etudes in the present work (pp. 52-60), they be introduced to the worthwhile scale and foundation studies of Pares, these two books being used in conjunction with one another from there on.

IF the *Modern Klose-Lazarus* proves itself a boon to those in quest of material to aid in solving the many involved problems that confront the present day instructors of clarinet, whether they be private teachers of the instrument, or public school music directors, the writer will feel gratified to know that his earnest efforts have been of at least some educational significance.

**Harvey S. Whistler**

# Preparatory Studies
## In the Low (Chalumeau) Register

### THE FIRST TONES
Half note (𝅗𝅥) = two counts—Whole note (𝅝) = four counts

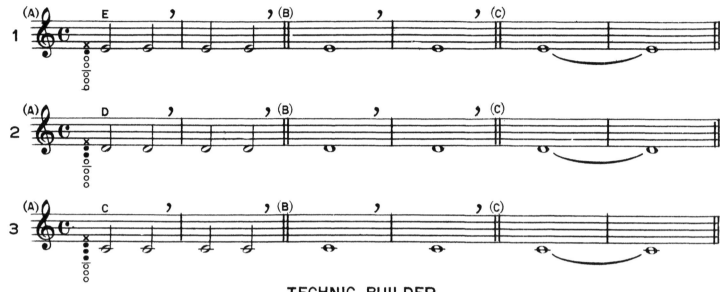

### TECHNIC BUILDER
Quarter note (♩) = one count

### EXTENDING THE RANGE UPWARD

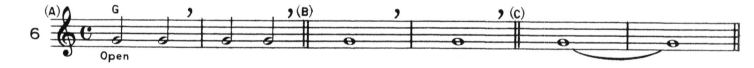

### TECHNIC BUILDER

## TONE STUDY

Whole Rest ( ➖ ) = 4 Counts

**9**

## THEME

Half Rest ( ➖ ) = 2 Counts

**10**

## FOLK SONG

**11**

## MELODIC AIR

**12**

## CAPRICE

Quarter Rest ( 𝄽 ) = 1 Count

**13**

## SONG WITHOUT WORDS

MENDELSSOHN

**14**

## EXCERPT from NINTH SYMPHONY

BEETHOVEN

**15**

# EXTENDING THE RANGE DOWNWARD

## LOW TONES

## TECHNIC BUILDER

## LARGO

## CHORALE STUDY

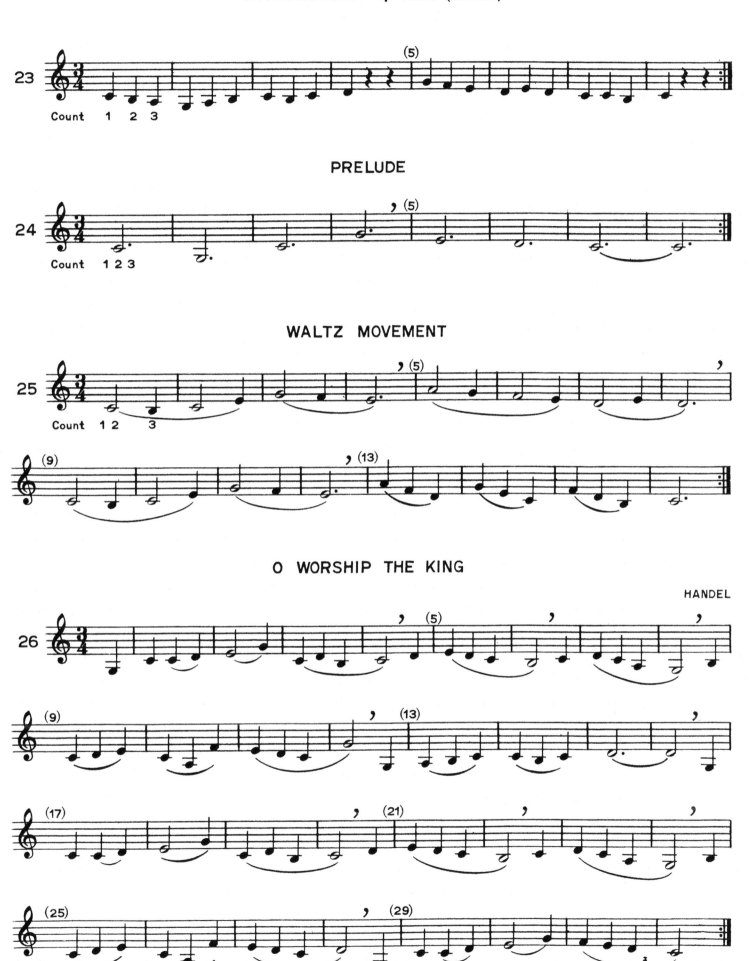

## INTRODUCING ¾ TIME (METER)

**23**

Count 1 2 3

## PRELUDE

**24**

Count 1 2 3

## WALTZ MOVEMENT

**25**

Count 1 2 3

## O WORSHIP THE KING

HANDEL

**26**

## LOWEST TONES

*When F is made with the small finger of the right hand, and E immediately follows, the E should be made with the small finger of the left hand, and vice versa.*

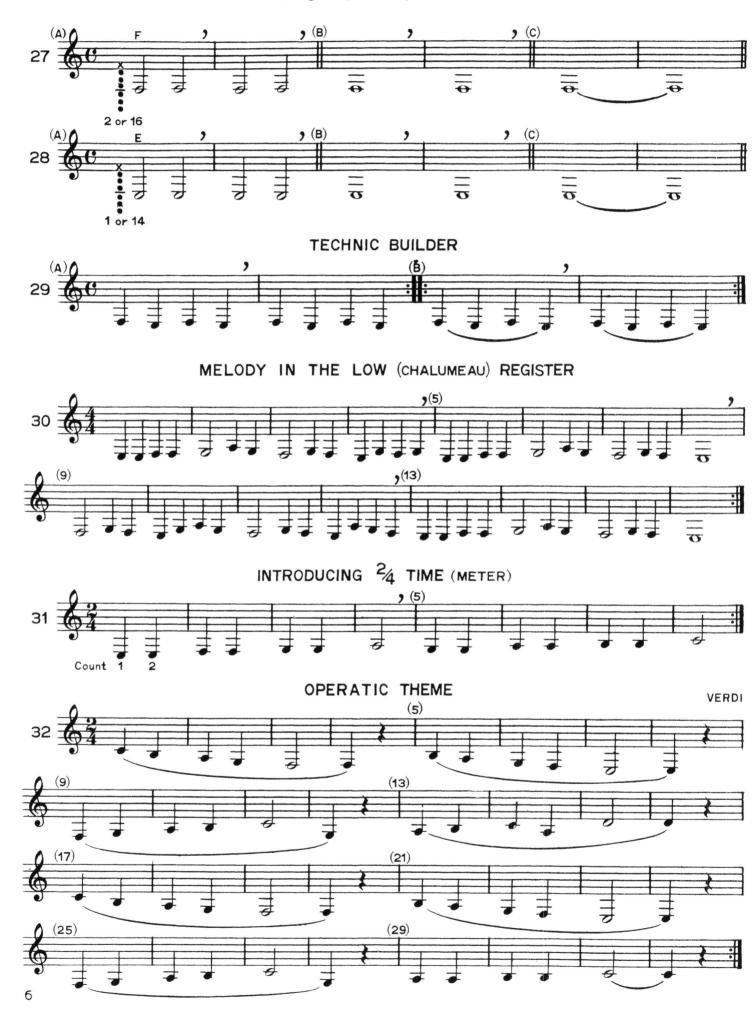

## TECHNIC BUILDER

## MELODY IN THE LOW (CHALUMEAU) REGISTER

## INTRODUCING 2/4 TIME (METER)

## OPERATIC THEME

VERDI

# Lazarus Foundation Studies

## CONNECTING THE RANGE

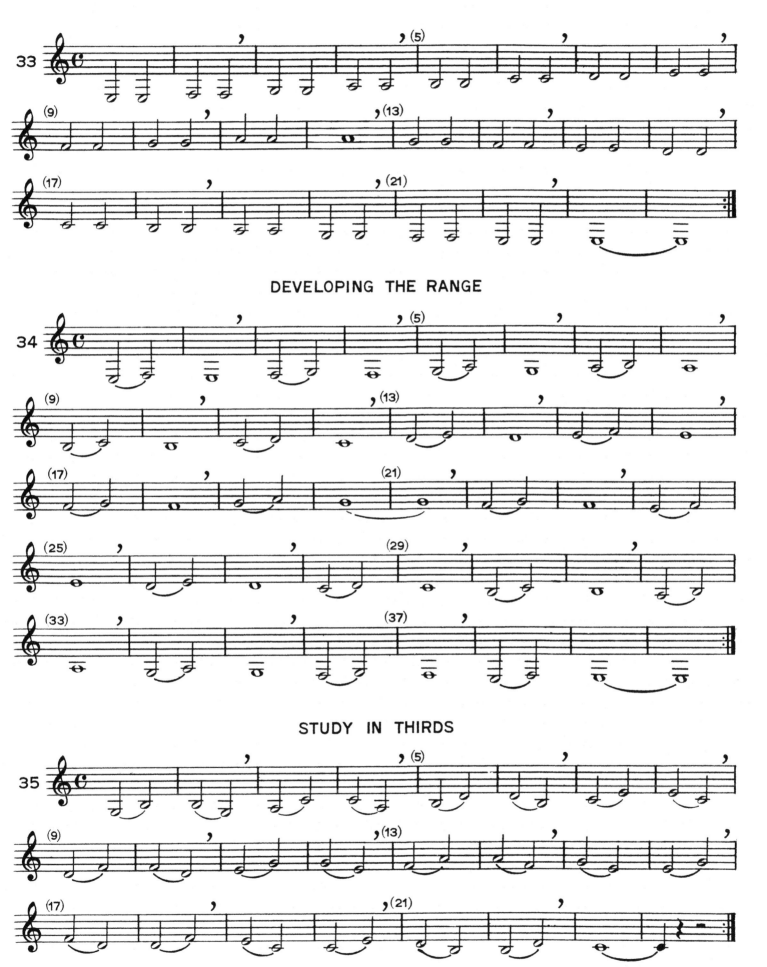

## DEVELOPING THE RANGE

## STUDY IN THIRDS

# Klose Tone Studies

Sustain a steady tone.

## SUSTAINED TONES

Hold each tone as long as possible.

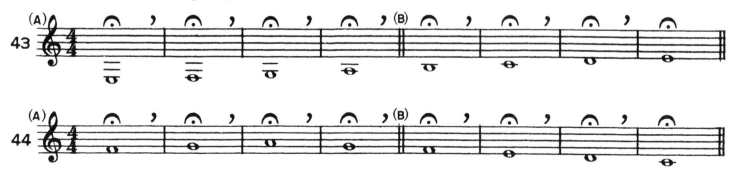

# Klose Embouchure Studies

Slur as many of the tones as possible in each section.

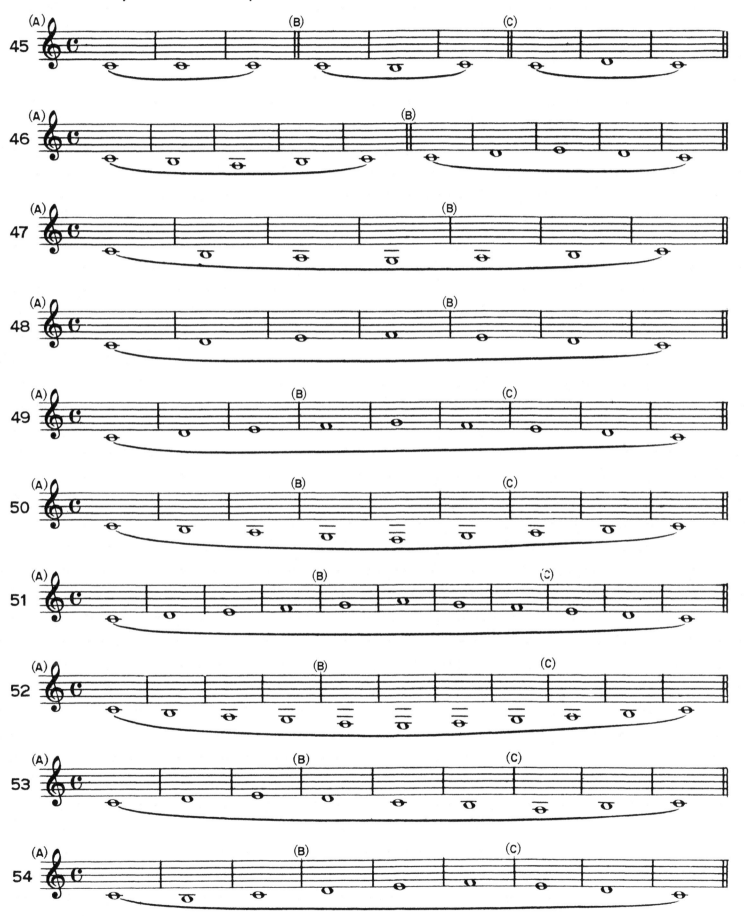

# From Low (Chalumeau) to Middle (Clarion) Register

## INTRODUCING THE REGISTER KEY

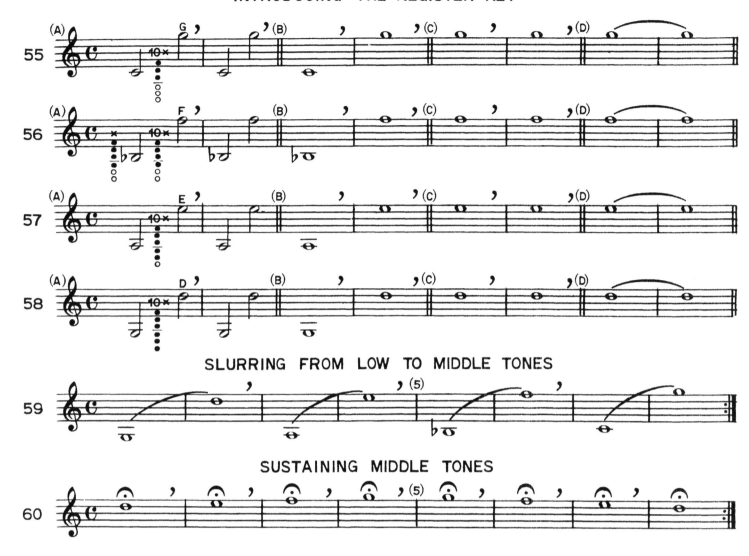

## SLURRING FROM LOW TO MIDDLE TONES

## SUSTAINING MIDDLE TONES

## OVER THE BREAK

*When C is made with the small finger of the right hand and B immediately follows, the B should be made with the small finger of the left hand, and vice versa.*

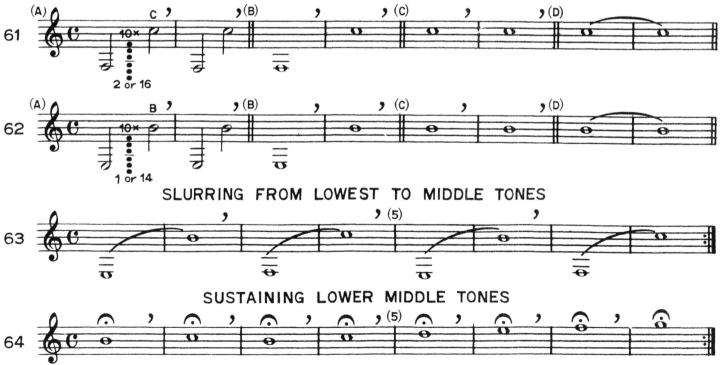

## SLURRING FROM LOWEST TO MIDDLE TONES

## SUSTAINING LOWER MIDDLE TONES

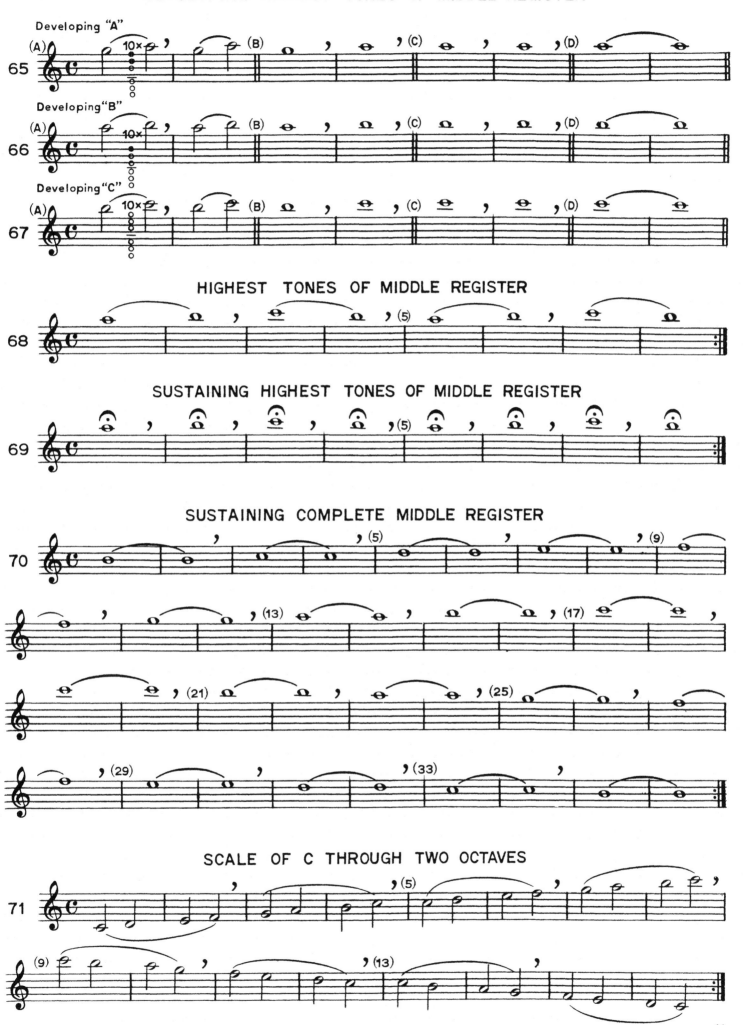

# EXERCISES ON THE BREAK

Repeat each exercise many times.

# EXERCISES GOING OVER THE BREAK

Repeat each exercise many times.

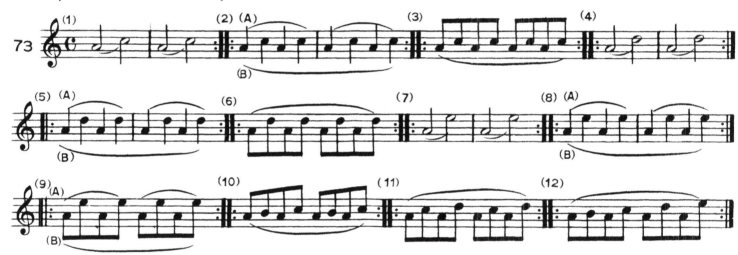

# VALSE LENTO

(Melody playable in **both** Low and Middle Registers)

Practice both parts

# Klose Interval Studies

## TO DEVELOP LEGATO PLAYING, INTONATION AND EMBOUCHURE

13

# Key of C Major

At this stage of advancement the student should, in addition to continuing the present study of Major key lessons in a systematic fashion, turn to page 37 and participate in the playing of duets. It is intended that the selected duets offered in the present volumn be studied concurrently with the Major key lessons from here on.

Scale of C. (Practice both parts.)    Chord of C

**82**

Also practice very slowly, holding each tone for (1) FOUR counts and (2) EIGHT counts.
When playing long tones, practice (1) ⟺ and (2) ⟺.

## SHORT EXERCISES IN C MAJOR

Repeat each exercise many times.

**83**

**84**

## INTRODUCING EIGHTH NOTES

Andante

**85**

Count    1 & 2 &

## STUDY IN EIGHTH NOTES
### (2/4 Meter)

Andantino

**86**

Count    1 & 2 &

## EXERCISE IN EIGHTH NOTES
### (4/4 Meter)

Moderato

**87**

Count    1 & 2 & 3 & 4 &

## QUARTER AND EIGHTH NOTES ALTERNATED

Moderato

**88**

## INTRODUCING STACCATO TONGUING

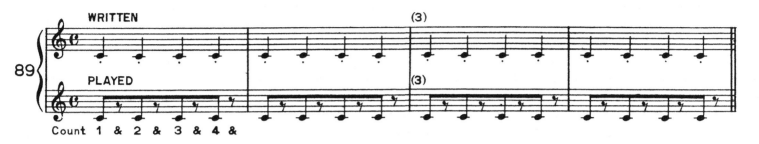

**89**

Count 1 & 2 & 3 & 4 &

## DEVELOPING THE STACCATO

Accent the first note of each pair; then strike the other note sharply and evenly, but with less force.

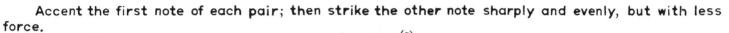

**90**

**91**

## STACCATO EXERCISE ON THE SCALE

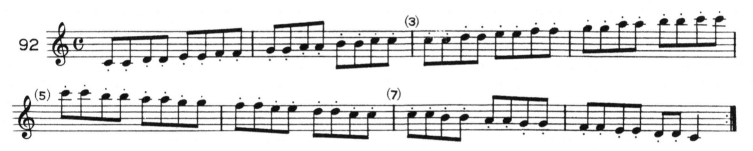

**92**

## STACCATO STUDY ON THE SCALE

**93**

# Key of G Major

NEW TONES

Thumb
hole
open

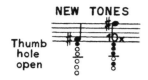

Scale of G. (Practice both parts.)          Chord of G

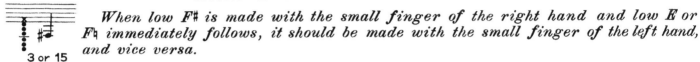

**94**

Also practice very slowly, holding each tone for (1) FOUR counts and (2) EIGHT counts.
When playing long tones, practice (1) ⤙ and (2) ⤙⤚ .

## SHORT EXERCISES IN G MAJOR

3 or 15

*When low F♯ is made with the small finger of the right hand and low E or F♮ immediately follows, it should be made with the small finger of the left hand, and vice versa.*

**95**   (A)   (♯) Repeat each exercise many times.   (B)   (♯)

**96**   (A)   (♯)   (B)   (♯)

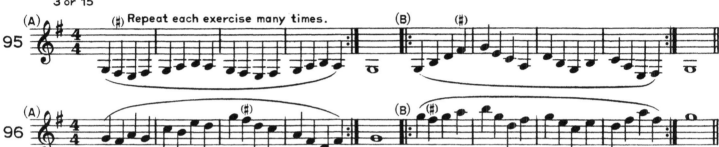

## ALLEGRETTO

BEHR

**97**   Brillante   (5)
mf

(9)   (13)

## Introducing the Dotted Quarter Note
## Followed by an Eighth Note

**98**   Moderato   (5)

Count 1 2   &

## ODE TO THE FOREST

GILLET

**99**   Dolce   (5)

Count 1 2 & 3

(9)   (13)

# EVENING PRAYER

HEROLD

100

# Largo from New World Symphony

DVORAK

101

# Key of F Major

**9 and 10 with thumb hole open**

Scale of F. (Practice both parts.)  Chord of F

**102**

Also practice very slowly, holding each tone for (1) FOUR counts and (2) EIGHT counts.
When playing long tones, practice (1) ◁ and (2) ◁▷

## SHORT EXERCISES IN F MAJOR

Repeat each exercise many times.

**103**

**104**

10x 7 or 17

## EVENTIDE

MENDELSSOHN

Cantabile

**105**

mp

(9)   (13)

(17)   (21)

mf

(25)   (29)

## SOLDIERS' CHORUS
from Fra Diavolo

AUBER

Marziale

**106**

f

(5)   (7)

# FINALE from ORPHEUS

OFFENBACH

# Melody in F

RUBENSTEIN

# Key of D Major

**Scale of D**          **Chord of D**

**(A)**        **(B)**

**109**

Also practice very slowly, holding each tone for (1) FOUR counts and (2) EIGHT counts.
When playing long tones, practice (1) ⎯⎯ and (2) ⎯⎯ ⎯⎯.

## SHORT EXERCISES IN D MAJOR

Repeat each exercise many times.

**110**

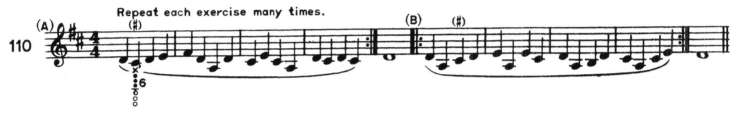

*When third space C♯ is made with the small finger of the right hand and B or C♮ immediately follows, it should be made with the small finger of the left hand, and vice versa.*

**111**

## INTRODUCING 3/8 TIME (METER)

Moderato

**112**

Count   1   2   3    1 2    3                      1 2 3

## THEME
### from Hansel and Gretel

HUMPERDINCK

Allegretto

**113**

## INTRODUCING ⁶⁄₈ TIME (METER)

**114** Adagio

Count 1 2 3 4 5 6  12 3 45 6  (3)  4 5 6

## RHYTHMICAL STUDY

**115** Moderato

Count 123456  (5)

# Nocturne

VON BLON

**116** Elegante

*mp*

(5)  (9)

(13)

(17)  *mf*

(21)

(25)

(29)

# Key of B♭ Major

### Scale of B♭. (Practice both parts.)  Chord of B♭

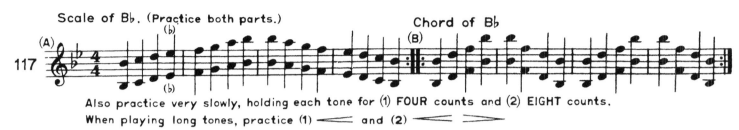

**(A)** 117 **(B)**

Also practice very slowly, holding each tone for (1) FOUR counts and (2) EIGHT counts.
When playing long tones, practice (1) ⟨⟩ and (2) ⟨⟩

## SHORT EXERCISES IN B♭ MINOR

Repeat each exercise many times.

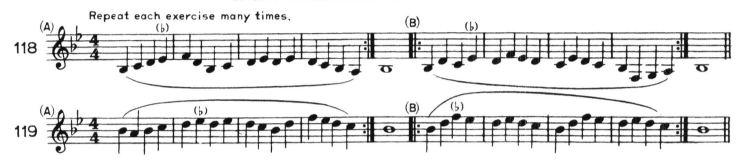

**(A)** 118 **(B)**

**(A)** 119 **(B)**

## INTRODUCING SIXTEENTH NOTES

### Moderato

120

Count 1 a & a    2 a & a    3 a & a    4 a & a

## STUDY IN SIXTEENTH NOTES

### Allegro ma non troppo

121  *mf*  (3)

(5)

(7)

## QUARTER AND SIXTEENTH NOTES ALTERNATED

### Allegro moderato

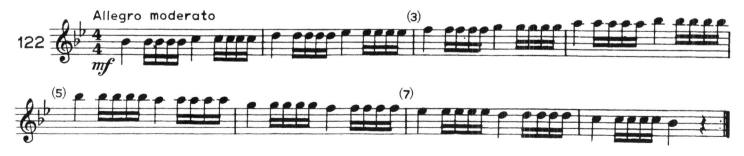

122  *mf*  (3)

(5)  (7)

24

## FIERCE FLAMES ARE RAGING
### from Il Trovatore

VERDI

## EXCERPT from STRADELLA

FLOTOW

## SONG WITHOUT WORDS

TSCHAIKOWSKY

# Key of A Major

Scale of A   (Practice both parts.)                    Chord of A

**126**

Also practice very slowly,  holding each tone for (1) FOUR counts and (2) EIGHT counts.

When playing long tones, practice (1) ⟨ and (2) ⟨ ⟩.

## SHORT EXERCISES IN A MAJOR

Repeat each exercise many times.

**127**

**128**

## IMPROMPTU, Op. 142

SCHUBERT

Cantabile

**129**

*mf*

## EXCERPT from L'ARLESIENNE SUITE

BIZET

Animato

**130**

*f*

## MELODY from OBERON

WEBER

Con spirito

**131**

*f*

# Introducing the Dotted Eighth Note
## Followed by A Sixteenth Note

**Moderato**

**132**

Count 1&a 2&a 3&a 4&a

## RHYTHMICAL STUDY

**Scherzando**

**133**

*mf*

## HUMORESKE THEME

DVORAK

**Grazioso**

**134**

*p*

## LA CZARINE

GANNE

**Allegro**

**135**

*f*

# Key of E♭ Major

Scale of E♭      Chord of E♭

136

With thumb hole open
Also practice very slowly, holding each tone for (1) FOUR counts and (2) EIGHT counts.
When playing long tones, practice (1) ◁ and (2) ◁ ▷

## SHORT EXERCISES IN E♭ MAJOR

Repeat each exercise many times.

137

138

## OPERATIC AIR

VERDI

Leggiero

139

## CONTRA DANCE

Giocoso

140

## MENUET from E♭ SYMPHONY

MOZART

Grazioso

141

# INTRODUCING TRIPLETS

## QUARTER NOTES AND TRIPLETS ALTERNATED

## PILGRIMS' CHORUS
### from Tannhauser

WAGNER

## ANDANTE
### from Fifth Symphony

TSCHAIKOWSKY

## SOLDIERS' CHORUS
### from Faust

GOUNOD

# Key of E Major

Scale of E (Practice both parts.)     Chord of E

**147**

Also practice very slowly, holding each tone for (1) FOUR counts and (2) EIGHT counts.
When playing long tones, practice (1) ——— and (2) ——— .

## SHORT EXERCISES IN E MAJOR
Repeat each exercise many times.

**148**

**149**

## SOLDIERS' MARCH
SCHUMANN

Ben marcato     (5)

**150**

(9)     (13)

## INTRODUCING SYNCOPATION

Moderato     (5)

**151**

Count 1 &2 &

(9)     (13)

## SONGS MY MOTHER TAUGHT ME
DVORAK

Affetuoso     (5) *R   R   R   R

**152**

1 &2     &

(9)     (13)

*R   R     (17)

* Use Right Hand Fingering for both tones on 17 and 18 Keyed Clarinets.

# SYNCOPATION STUDY

KUFFNER

Allegretto

153

Count 1  &2,  &3   &4   &

## FINALE, SECOND ACT OF ZAMPA
### (Tied Syncopation)

HEROLD

Allegro moderato

154

## ON WINGS OF SONG

MENDELSSOHN

Andante

155

rall.

# Key of A♭ Major

Scale of A♭ (Practice both parts.)    Chord of A♭

**156**

Also practice very slowly, holding each tone for (1) FOUR counts and (2) EIGHT counts.
When playing long tones, practice (1) ⊲ and (2) ⊲ ⊳

## SHORT EXERCISES IN A♭ MAJOR

Repeat each exercise many times.

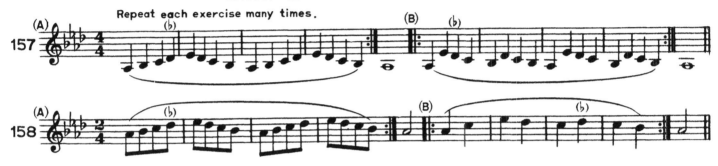

**157**

**158**

## PROCESSIONAL MARCH

HAYDN

**159** Grandioso

## NIGHTFALL

FRANZ ABT

**160** Affetuoso

## EXCERPT from IL TROVATORE

VERDI

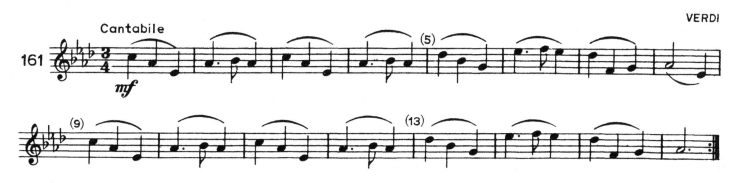

## EIGHTEENTH CENTURY THEME

MOZART

## MEDITATION

THOME

*D. S. al fine*

# Chromatic Scale
## In the Low (Chalumeau) Register

Also practice very slowly, holding each tone for (1) EIGHT counts, and (2) SIXTEEN counts.

When playing long tones, practice (1) ⟨ and (2) ⟨⟩.

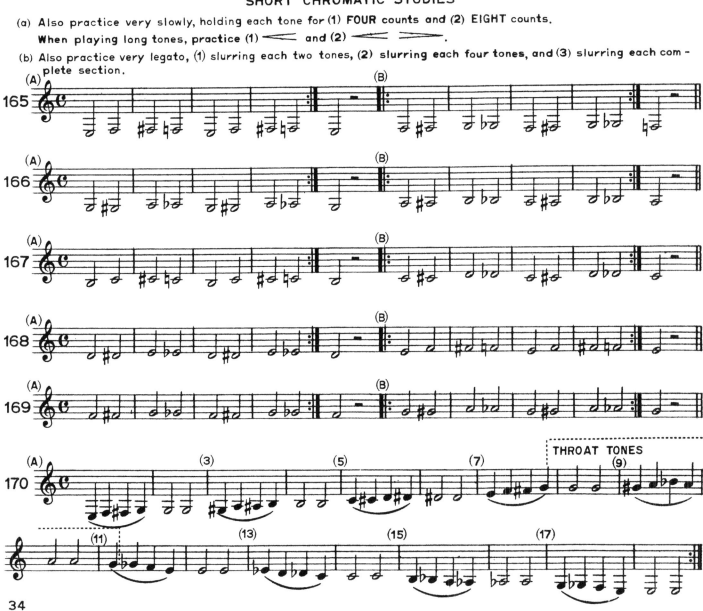

KNOWN AS "THROAT TONES"

9 and 10 with thumb hole open

Thumb hole open

3 or 15

## SHORT CHROMATIC STUDIES

(a) Also practice very slowly, holding each tone for (1) FOUR counts and (2) EIGHT counts.

When playing long tones, practice (1) ⟨ and (2) ⟨⟩.

(b) Also practice very legato, (1) slurring each two tones, (2) slurring each four tones, and (3) slurring each complete section.

THROAT TONES

# Chromatic Scale

## In the Middle (Clarion) Register

Also practice very slowly, holding each tone for (1) EIGHT counts, and (2) SIXTEEN counts.
When playing long tones, practice (1) and (2)

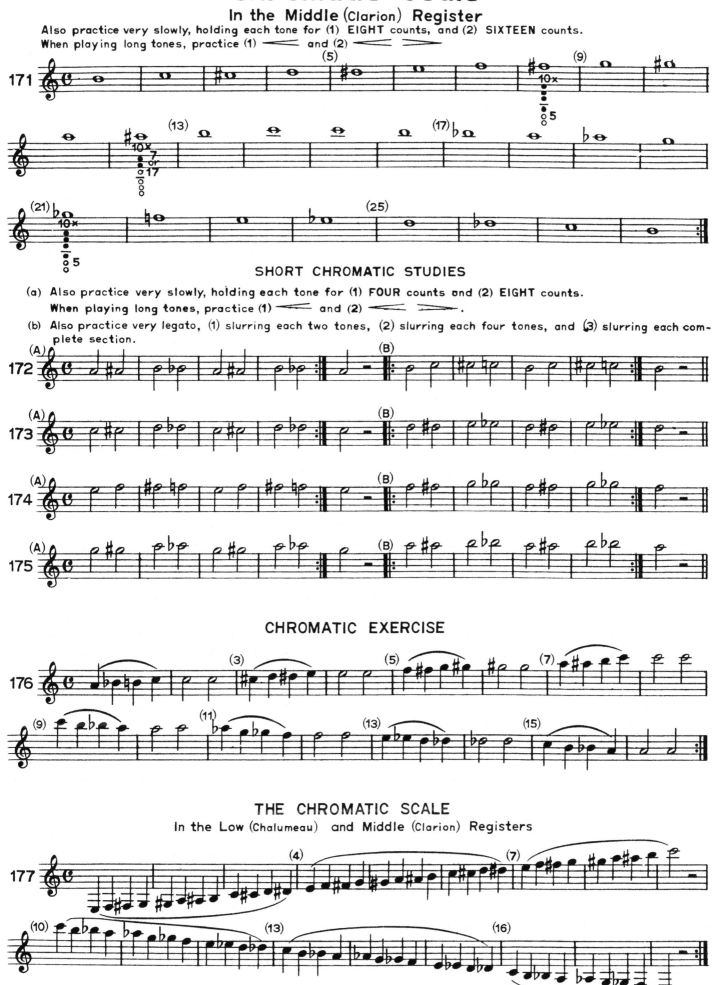

## SHORT CHROMATIC STUDIES

(a) Also practice very slowly, holding each tone for (1) FOUR counts and (2) EIGHT counts.
When playing long tones, practice (1) and (2) .

(b) Also practice very legato, (1) slurring each two tones, (2) slurring each four tones, and (3) slurring each complete section.

## CHROMATIC EXERCISE

## THE CHROMATIC SCALE

### In the Low (Chalumeau) and Middle (Clarion) Registers

# Lazarus Studies Introducing Alla Breve (Cut) Time

Alla Breve (Cut) Time is 4/4 Time (Meter) with TWO BEATS to the measure instead of four
It is Indicated by the sign ₡

# Clarinet Duets

Selected from the works of Lazarus, Spohr, Kuffner and others.

Duets should be practiced with a variety of tonal shadings $(p, mp, mf, f)$.

### FIRST DUET IN COMMON OR ALLA BREVE TIME
(Before playing Duets in Alla Breve Time, carefully
study this procedure as illustrated on page 36.)

LAZARUS

### SECOND DUET IN COMMON OR ALLA BREVE TIME

LAZARUS

### WALTZ IN DUET STYLE

LAZARUS

## THIRD DUET IN COMMON OR ALLA BREVE TIME

LAZARUS

## DUET IN ²⁄₄ TIME

LAZARUS

## CLASSICAL WALTZ MOVEMENT

LAZARUS

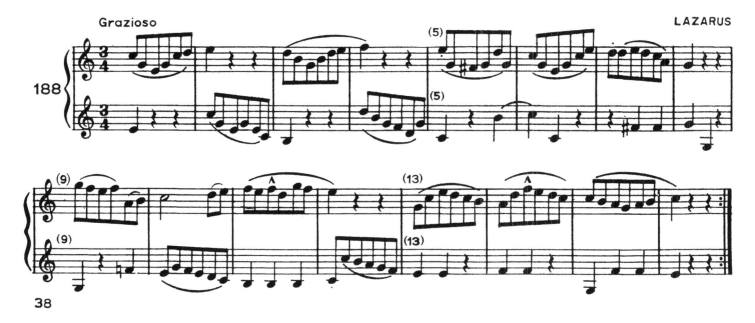

## TECHNICAL CAPRICE

KUFFNER

## RHYTHMICAL CAPRICE

KUFFNER

## AN EIGHTEENTH CENTURY THEME

MOZART

## LEGATO DUET

LAZARUS

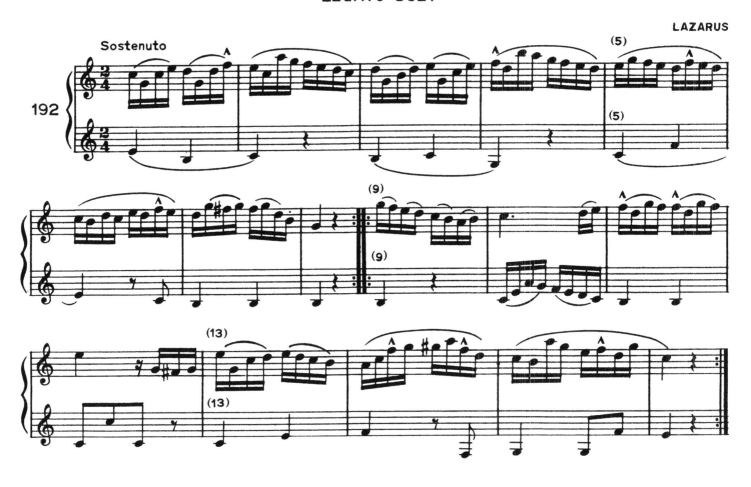

## STACCATO DUET

LAZARUS

# RHYTHMICAL DUET IN COMMON OR ALLA BREVE TIME

LAZARUS

## Air from Rigoletto

VERDI

# Rolling Stones

SPOHR

# Londonderry Air

TRADITIONAL

# TRADITIONAL DUET IN COMMON OR ALLA BREVE TIME

KUFFNER

# DUET IN 6/8 TIME

KUFFNER

## CHARACTERISTIC EPISODE

KUFFNER

# ARTISTIC DUET

KUFFNER

## Viennese Melody

TRADITIONAL

# CONCERT THEME IN DUET FORM

KUFFNER

# Cavatina

SPOHR

204

# Excerpt from Zampa

HEROLD

205

# Symphonic Processional

ROSSINI

# Operatic Aria

DONIZETTI

# Klose Exercises in Mechanism

For the Development of Agility, Speed and Equality of Fingering.

# Etude in C Major

At this stage of advancement the student should, in addition to continuing the present study of Etudes in a systematic fashion, turn to page 61 and become acquainted with the art of cross fingering and the production of tones in the upper register of his instrument. A portion of the daily practice should now be devoted to playing long tones and other suitable materials in the high register of the clarinet.

Articulations to be practiced.

LAZARUS

# Etude in G

LAZARUS

# Etude in F

**Articulations to be practiced.**

BERR

Allegro

211

# Etude in D

LAZARUS

# Etude in B♭

LAZARUS

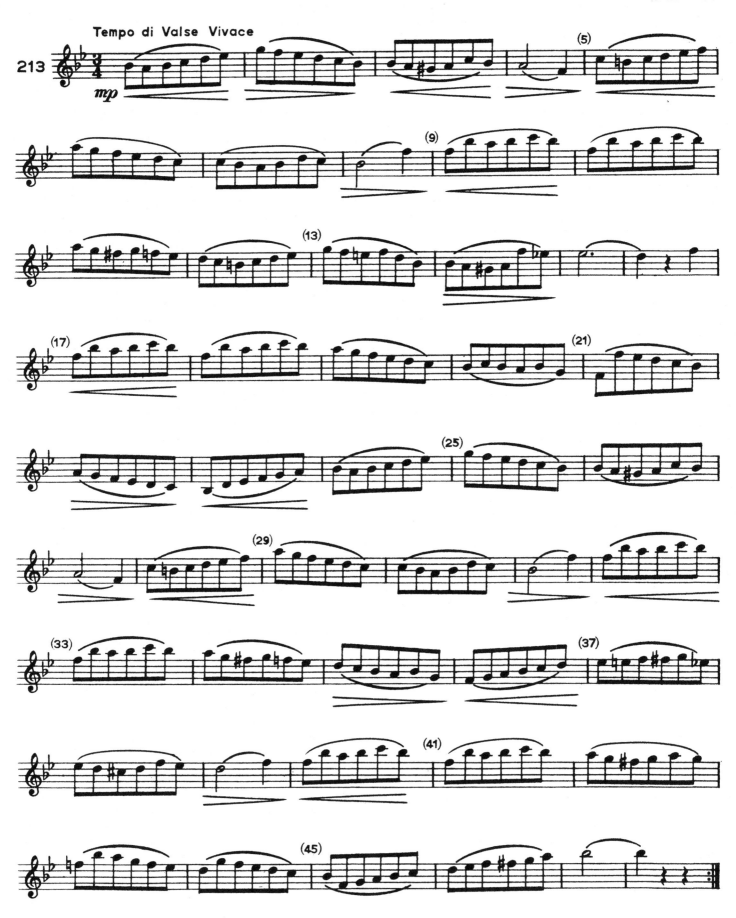

# Etude in A

TRADITIONAL

# Etude in E♭

KLOSE

Allegretto
Play entire Etude as indicated in first two measures.

215

*mf*
*staccato*

# Etude in E

KLOSE

Before playing this etude review Syncopation Studies Nos. 151, 153, 154, as well as Dvorak's "Songs My Mother Taught Me," No 152, all found in lesson in Key of E Major, pages 30-31.

# Etude in A♭

KLOSE

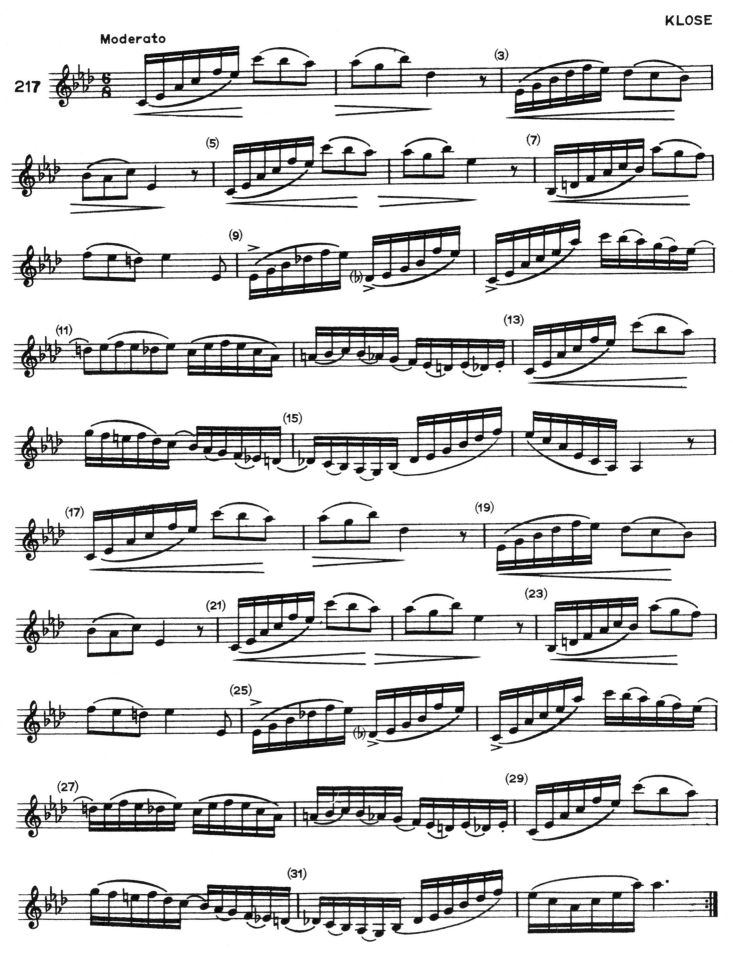

# High (Altissimo) Register of the Clarinet
## INTRODUCTION TO CROSS FINGERING

The flatness of pitch common in clarinet sections of many bands when playing in the upper register of the instrument is due to a lack of attention being paid to the study of this particular register of the clarinet. The systematic practice of both long tones and slurs in the upper register of the instrument is indispensible if the student is to play true to pitch. When playing high tones on the clarinet it is of paramount importance that they be played with a firm, secure embouchure.

### "C#"-"Db"

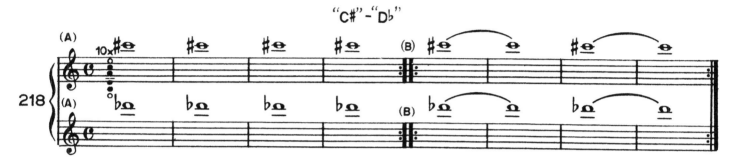

### INTRODUCING "D"

*To produce a true, bright tone, it is necessary on most clarinets to press key No. 4 when playing D above the staff as well as some of the tones higher than D. (See Modern Klose-Lazarus Fingering Chart.)*

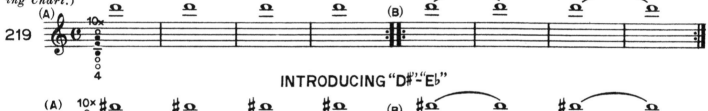

### INTRODUCING "D#"-"Eb"

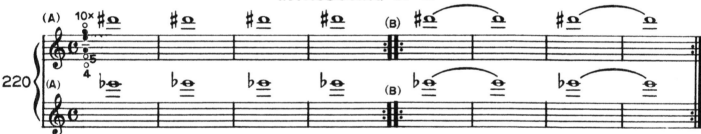

### INTRODUCING "E"

### CHROMATIC EXERCISE

### DEVELOPING HIGH TONES

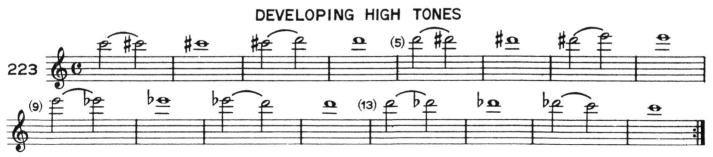

## SLURRING HIGH TONES

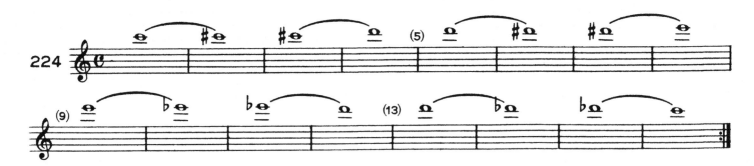

## SHORT STUDIES IN THE HIGH REGISTER

(a) Also practice very slowly, holding each tone for (1) FOUR counts, and (2) EIGHT counts.
When playing long tones, practice (1) ⤙ and (2) ⤙⤚ .

(b) Also practice very legato, (1) slurring each two tones, (2) slurring each four tones, and (3) slurring each eight tones.

## SUSTAINING HIGH TONES

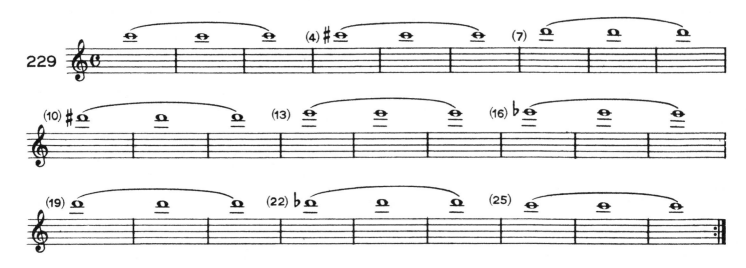

## INTRODUCING "F"

## INTRODUCING "F#" – "G♭"

## INTRODUCING "G"

## CHROMATIC EXERCISE

## DEVELOPING HIGH TONES

## SLURRING HIGH TONES

## SHORT STUDIES IN THE HIGH REGISTER

(a) Also practice very slowly, holding each tone for (1) FOUR counts, and (2) EIGHT counts.
When playing long tones, practice (1) ⟍ and (2) ⟍ ⟋ .
(b) Also practice very legato, (1) slurring each two tones, (2) slurring each four tones, and (3) slurring each eight tones.

## SUSTAINING HIGH TONES

# Major Scales Extending into the High Register

**Articulations to be played.**

Also practice very slowly, holding each tone for (1) FOUR counts and (2) EIGHT counts.
When playing long tones, practice (1) ⟨ and (2) ⟨⟩

## SLURS IN THE HIGH REGISTER

Repeat each exercise many times.

# Major Scales in Thirds

Articulations to be played.

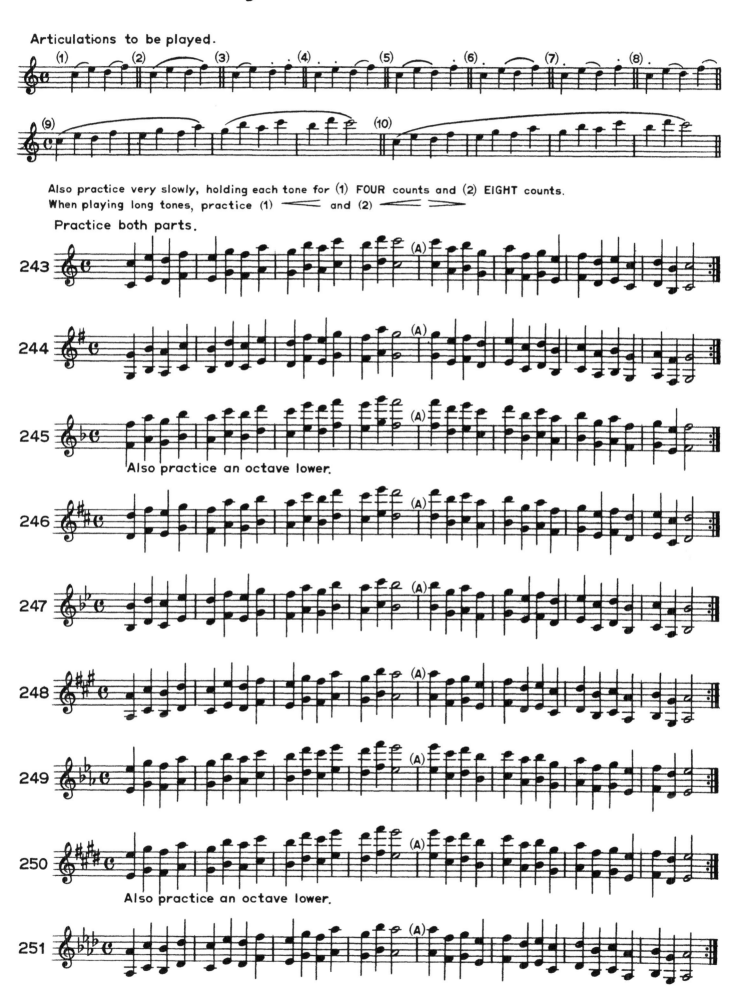

Also practice very slowly, holding each tone for (1) FOUR counts and (2) EIGHT counts.
When playing long tones, practice (1) and (2)

Practice both parts.

Also practice an octave lower.

Also practice an octave lower.

# Melodies in the High Register

O WORSHIP THE KING

HANDEL

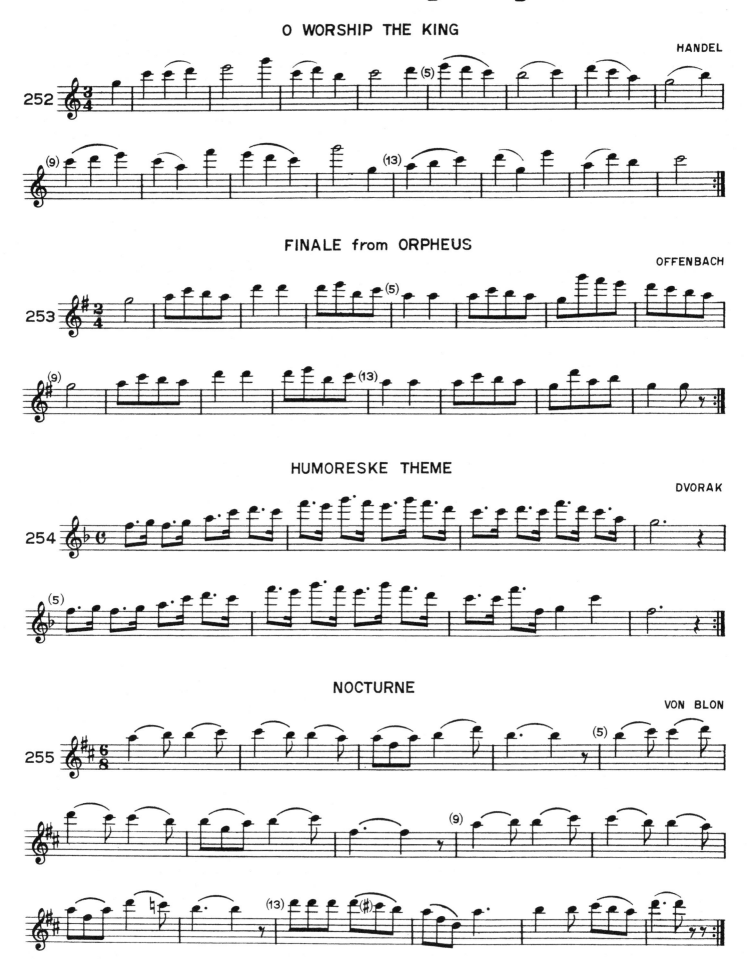

FINALE from ORPHEUS

OFFENBACH

HUMORESKE THEME

DVORAK

NOCTURNE

VON BLON

# Tone Studies in the High Register

Sustain tone for sixteen counts.

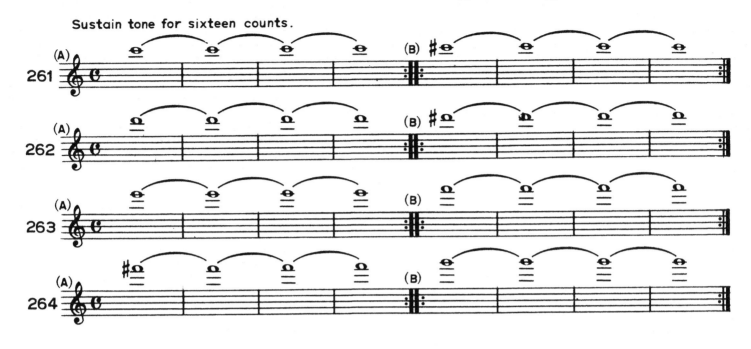

## CAPRICE IN THE HIGH REGISTER

LAZARUS

## ETUDE IN THE HIGH REGISTER

LAZARUS

# Musical Embellishments (Ornamentation)

The APPOGGIATURA (sometimes called Long Grace Note or Classical Grace Note) is a small ornamental note receiving half of the time value of the note before which it is placed. In the music of the old masters frequent use was made of this type of embellishment.

WRITTEN

PLAYED

Observe that the accent falls on the embellishment rather than on the note to which it is attached.

### EXCERPT FROM SERENADE
(Using the Appoggiatura)

HAYDN

The ACCIACCATURA (sometimes called Short Appoggiatura, Short Grace Note, or Modern Grace Note) is a small ornamental note written with a line through its stem. It is played quickly and its time value is taken from that of the note preceding it rather than from that of the note to which it is attached. It is an embellishment used by the old masters; in addition, it is the type of grace note most frequently employed by modern composers.

WRITTEN

PLAYED

Observe that the accent falls on the principal note rather than on the embellishment.

### EXCERPT FROM GAVOTTE
(Using the Acciaccatura)

GOSSEC

### EXCERPT FROM CHANT SANS PAROLES
(Using the Acciaccatura)

TSCHAIKOWSKY

# MELODY
(Using both the Appoggiatura and the Acciaccatura)

TOURS

Whenever double grace notes or groups of three or more ornamental notes occur in music, the accent or stress should fall upon the principal note to which they are attached.

# ORNAMENTAL THEME
(Using both double grace notes and groups of grace notes)

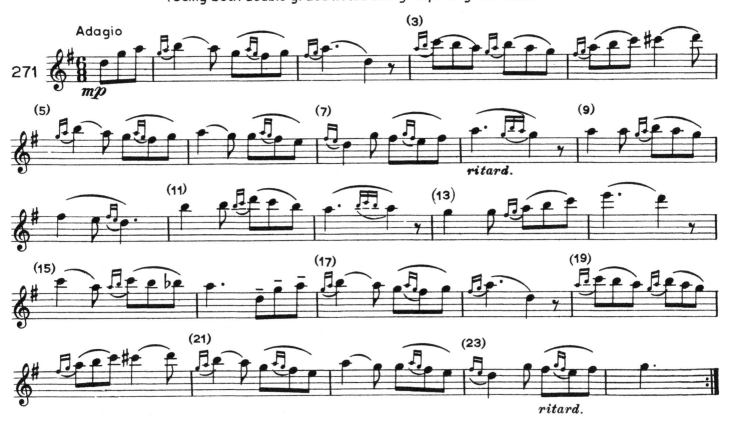

The MORDANT (sometimes called a Passing Shake) is, in its most commonly played form, a double grace note embellishment consisting of the principal note alternated with a note above it. The sign ∿ placed over a note indicates the mordant, and when an accidental is placed over this sign the second note of the embellishment must be so altered.

## MORDANTS AFFECTED BY ACCIDENTALS

## MORDANT STUDY

## EXERCISE USING THE MORDANT

\* Use trill fingering.   See Modern Klose-Lazarus Table of Trills.

The GRUPETTO (popularly known as a Turn) is a musical ornament consisting of a group of notes formed by taking the adjoining notes above and below the principal note, according to its position in the diatonic scale. It is indicated by the sign ∽ and is used in different ways.

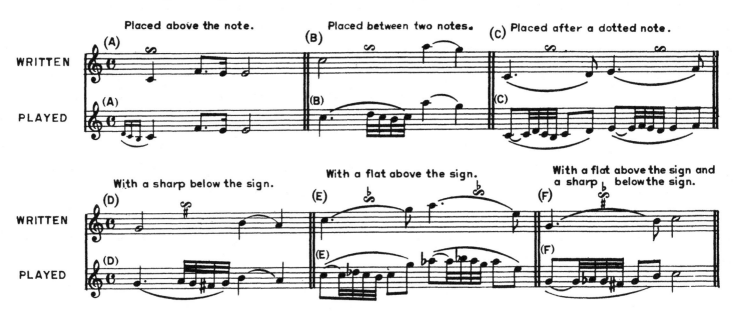

## GRUPETTO STUDY

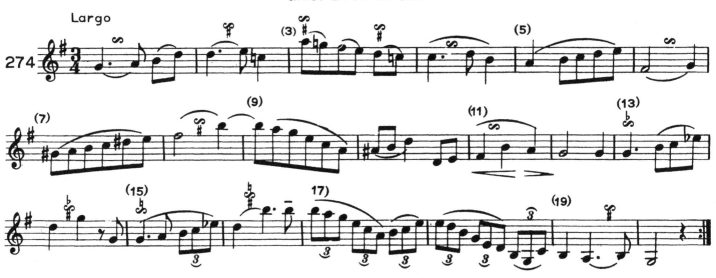

## MARCH OF THE GYPSIES
### from Preciosa

Von WEBER

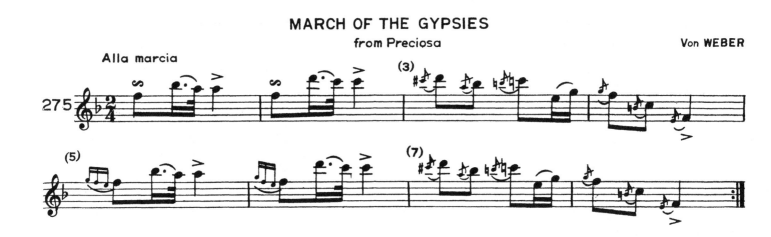

The TRILL (sometimes called a Shake) is the most commonly used embellishment in music. It is an ornamental effect produced by the rapid and regular alterations of two tones, either a whole step or a half-step apart, and is indicated by the letters *tr* above the principal note, the alternate note being the one above it. It does not matter how many notes a trill contains; the greater the number of notes in a trill, the more life and brilliancy the embellishment will radiate.

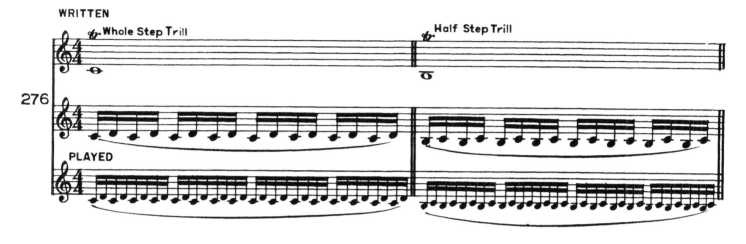

The Trill ending with grace notes.    The Trill ending without grace notes.

If it is necessary to sharpen or flatten the alternate notes of a trill, a ♯ or ♭ is placed above the *tr*.

If it is intended that the trill begin with the alternate note instead of the principal note, an acciaccatura is placed before the principal note.

# Trill Study

KLOSE

# Embellished Melody

LAZARUS

# Long Trill Etude

BERR

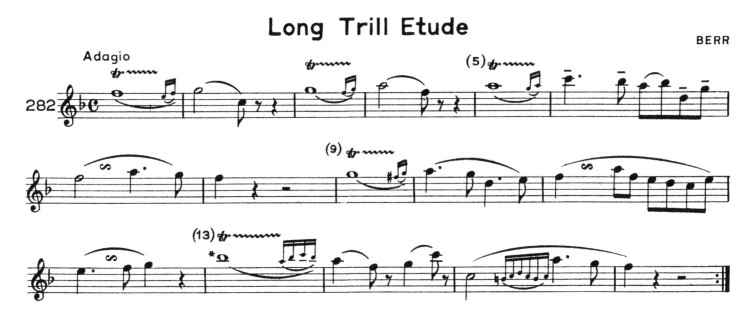

* Trill fingering is given on Modern Klose-Lazarus Table of Trills.

# Basic Trill Exercises

Trill fingerings are given on Modern Klose-Lazarus Table of Trills

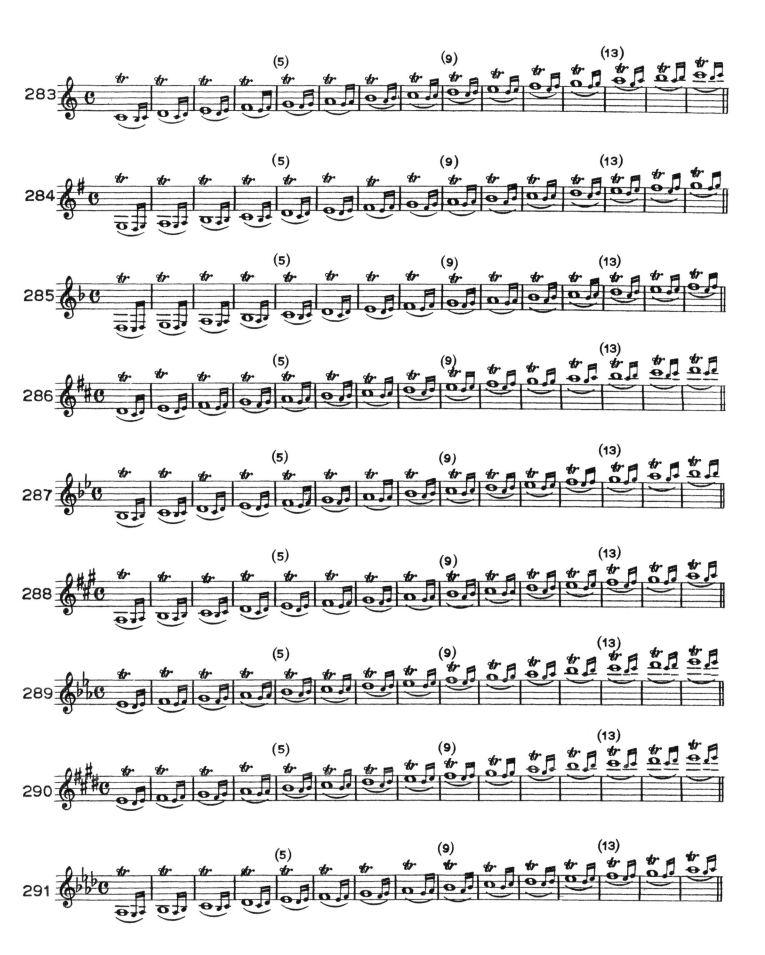

# Key of A Minor

(Relative to the Key of C Major)

Scale of A Harmonic Minor. (Practice both parts.) Scale of A Melodic Minor

Also practice very slowly, holding each tone for (1) FOUR counts and (2) EIGHT counts.
When playing long tones, practice (1) ⎯⎯ and (2) ⎯⎯⎯⎯.

## EXERCISE IN A MINOR

Moderato

## ROMANZA

SPOHR

Grazioso

## CHANSON TRISTE

TSCHAIKOWSKY

Con dolore

rit

# Key of E Minor
### (Relative to the Key of G Major)
Scale of E Harmonic Minor  (Practice both parts.)  Scale of E Melodic Minor

Also practice very slowly, holding each tone for (1) FOUR counts and (2) EIGHT Counts.
When playing long tones, practice (1) ⟨ and (2) ⟨ ⟩.

## EXERCISE IN E MINOR

## ELEGIE
MASSENET

## ELEGIE
### (An Octave Higher)
MASSENET

# Key of D Minor

### (Relative to the Key of F Major)

**Scale of D Harmonic Minor** (Practice both parts.) **Scale of D Melodic Minor**

Also practice very slowly, holding each tone for (1) FOUR counts and (2) EIGHT counts.
When playing long tones, practice (1) and (2)

## EXERCISE IN D MINOR

**Allegretto**

## CONSOLATION

SCHUMANN

**Cantabile**

## CONSOLATION

### (An Octave Higher)

SCHUMANN

**Cantabile**

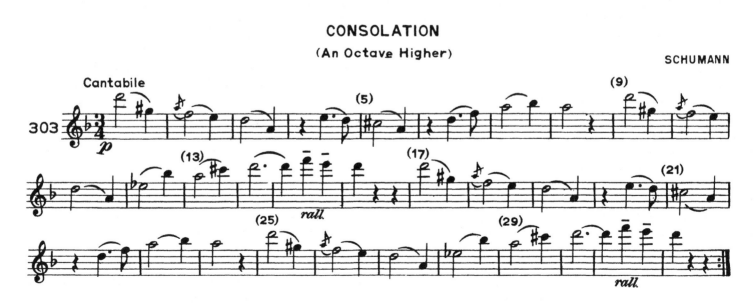

# Key of B Minor
## (Relative to the Key of D Major)

Scale of B Harmonic Minor (Practice both parts.)   Scale of B Melodic Minor

Also practice very slowly, holding each tone for (1) FOUR counts and (2) EIGHT counts.
When playing long tones, practice (1) ◁ and (2) ◁▷

## EXERCISE IN B MINOR

Moderato

## NIGHT WINDS

TSCHAIKOWSKY
Op. 30, No. 24

Agitato

## NIGHT WINDS
### (An Octave Higher)

TSCHAIKOWSKY
Op. 30, No. 24

Agitato

# Key of G Minor
(Relative to the Key of B♭ Major)

Scale of G Harmonic Minor  (Practice both parts.)  Scale of G Melodic Minor

Also practice very slowly, holding each tone for (1) FOUR counts and (2) EIGHT counts.
When playing long tones, practice (1) ◁ and (2) ◁ ▷.

## EXERCISE IN G MINOR

## SERENADE

SCHUBERT

# Key of F# Minor
## (Relative to the Key of A Major)

Scale of F# Harmonic Minor  (Practice both parts.)  Scale of F# Melodic Minor

(A)  (B)

**311**

Also practice very slowly, holding each tone for (1) FOUR counts and (2) EIGHT counts.
When playing long tones, practice (1) ⸺ and (2) ⸺.

## EXERCISE IN F# MINOR

Moderato

**312**

## ANDALUSIAN DANCE

GRANADOS

Allegro

**313**

## VALSETTE

GODARD

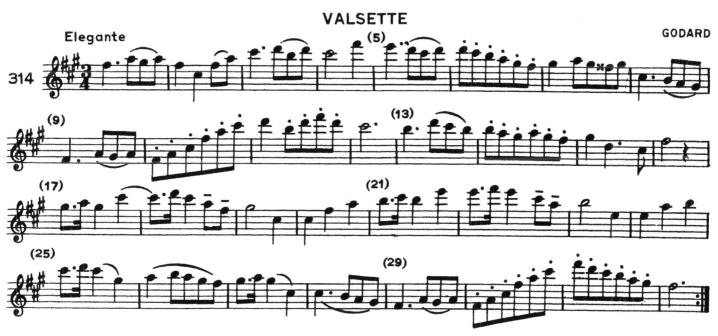

Elegante

**314**

# Key of C Minor

(Relative to the Key of E♭ Major)

Scale of C Harmonic Minor (Practice both parts.)    Scale of C Melodic Minor

Also practice very slowly, holding each tone for (1) FOUR counts and (2) EIGHT counts.
When playing long tones, practice (1) ◁ and (2) ◁

## EXERCISE IN C MINOR

## ORIENTALE

CESAR CUI
Op. 50

# Key of C# Minor
### (Relative to the Key of E Major)

Scale of C# Harmonic Minor  (Practice both parts.)     Scale of C# Melodic Minor

Also practice very slowly, holding each tone for (1) FOUR counts and (2) EIGHT counts.
When playing long tones, practice (1) ⟨⟩ and (2) ⟨⟩.

## EXERCISE IN C# MINOR

This is Exercise No. 316 from previous lesson, transposed from C Minor to C# Minor.

## ETUDE SYMPHONIQUE

A. CAMPANARI
Op.37, No. 8

# Key of F Minor
(Relative to the Key of A♭ Major)

Scale of F Harmonic Minor (Practice both parts.)  Scale of F Melodic Minor

**321**

Also practice very slowly, holding each tone for (1) FOUR counts and (2) EIGHT counts.
When playing long tones, practice (1) ——◁ and (2) ◁——▷

## EXERCISE IN F MINOR

Legato e sostenuto

**322**

## ETUDE SYMPHONIQUE

A. CAMPANARI
Op. 37, No. 9

Larghetto

**323**

\* On 17 and 18 Keyed Clarinets use Right Hand Fingering for the start of the tone C, immediately transfering its production to the left hand.

# Klose Articulation Studies

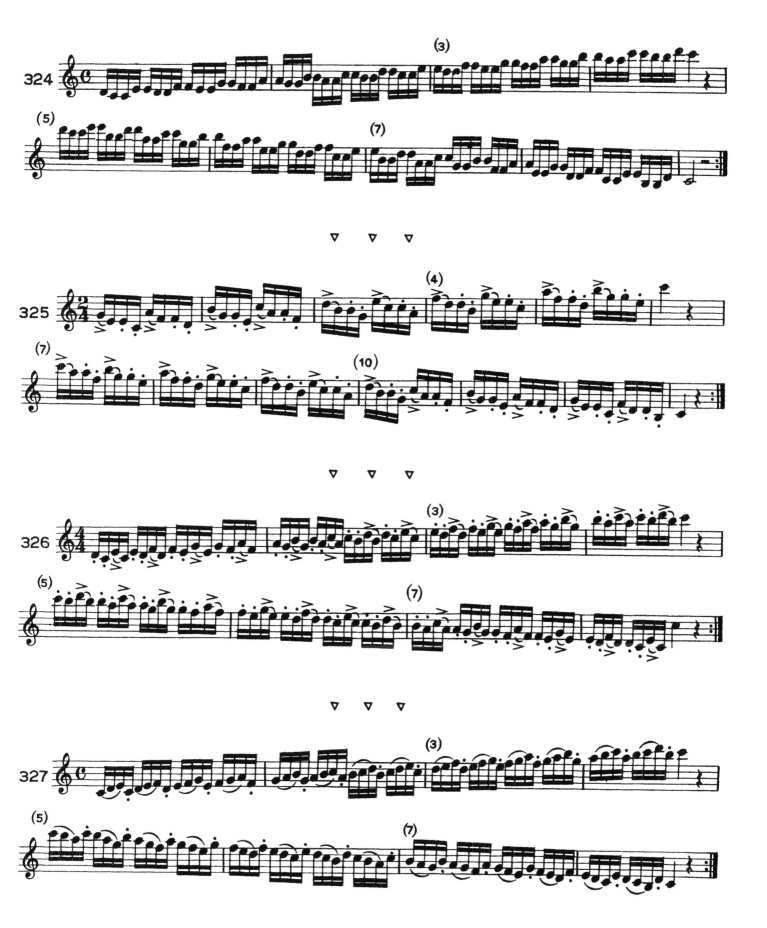

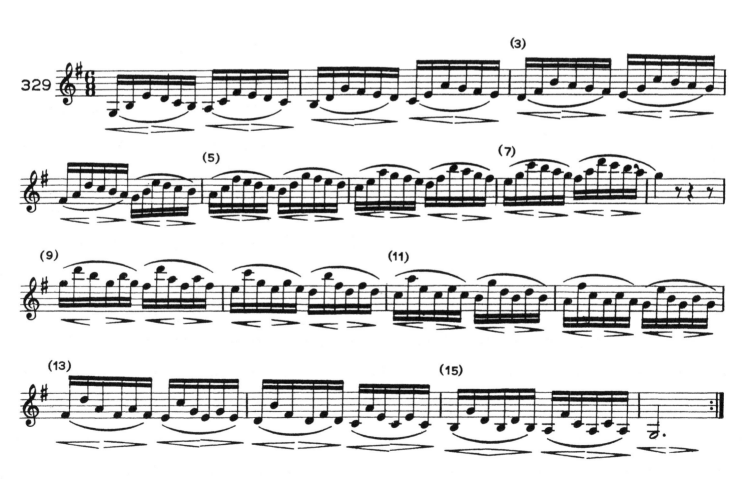

90

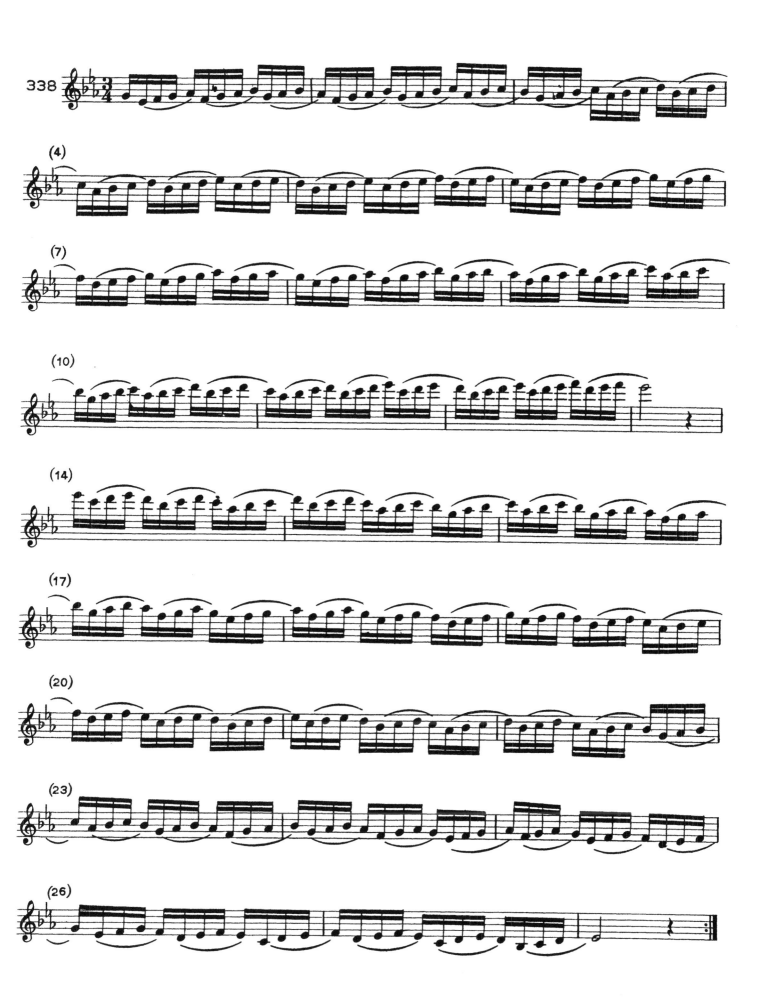

338

**Also practice slowly, tonguing and holding each tone for (1) ONE count and (2) FOUR counts.**

# Major, Minor and Chromatic Scales

## BASIC ARTICULATIONS
### (Staccato and Legato)

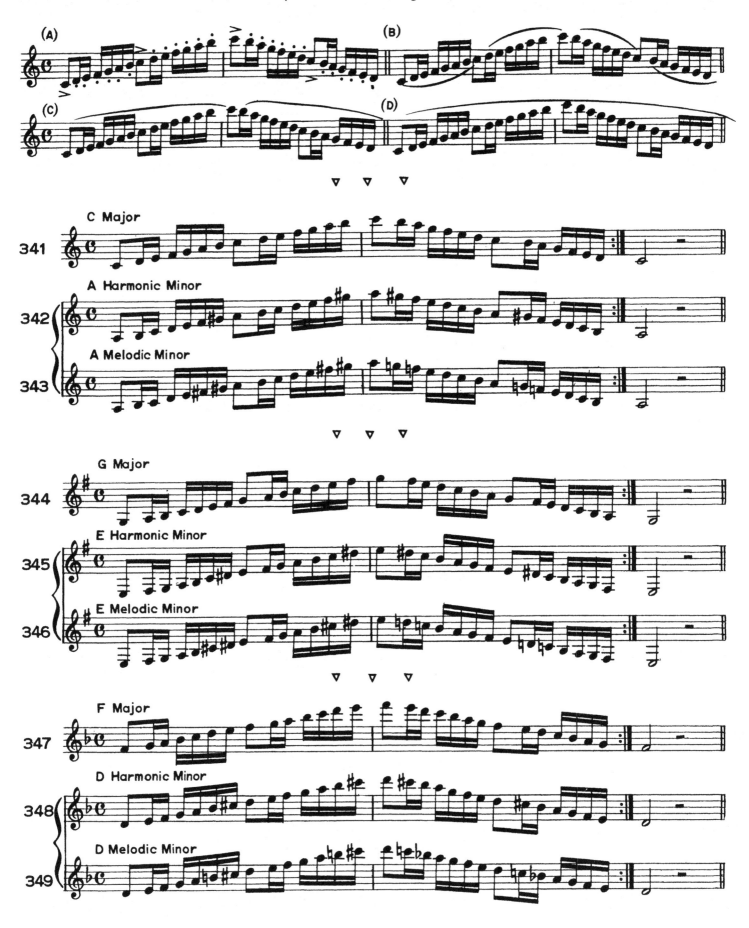

## CHROMATIC SCALES

Practice (1) tonguing each note staccato, (2) slurring each four measures, and (3) playing entire scale in one slur.

Practice (1) tonguing each note staccato, (2) slurring each three measures, and (3) playing entire scale in one slur.